KINGFISHER READERS

level 1

Busy as a Bee

Thea Feldman

KINGFISHER
NEW YORK

KINGFISHER
LONDON & NEW YORK

Copyright © Macmillan Publishers International Ltd 2012
Published in the United States by Kingfisher,
175 Fifth Ave., New York, NY 10010
Kingfisher is an imprint of Macmillan Children's Books, London.
All rights reserved.

Distributed in the U.S. and Canada by Macmillan,
175 Fifth Ave., New York, NY 10010

Library of Congress Cataloging-in-Publication data
has been applied for.

Series editor: Thea Feldman
Literacy consultant: Ellie Costa, Bank St. School for Children, New York

ISBN: 978-0-7534-6899-9 (HB)
ISBN: 978-0-7534-6900-2 (PB)

Kingfisher books are available for special promotions
and premiums. For details contact: Special Markets
Department, Macmillan, 175 Fifth Ave.,
New York, NY 10010.

For more information, please visit
www.kingfisherbooks.com

Printed in China
9 8 7 6 5
5TR/0516/WKT/UG/105MA

Picture credits
The Publisher would like to thank the following for permission to reproduce their material.
Top = t; Bottom = b; Center = c; Left = l; Right = r
Cover Shutterstock/Nikita Tiunov; 3 Shutterstock/Daniel Prudeck; 4-5 Getty/Superstock; 6–7 Shutterstock/
chantal de bruijne; 8 Shutterstock/Jasenka; 8–9 Getty/Corbis Bridge; 10-11 Shutterstock/Klayivik; 12 Alamy/
Imagebroker; 12-13 Shutterstock/Nikola Spasenoski; 14 Getty/Peter Arnold; 15 Naturepl/Kim Taylor;
16–17 Frank Lane Picture Agency (FLPA)/Horst Solliger/Imagebroker; 18–19 Getty/P&R Fotos; 20 FLPA/
Mark Moffet/Minden; 21 Getty/Phototake Science; 22 Getty/OSF; 23 Naturepl/Laurent Geslin; 24 Getty/OSF;
25 Specialist Stock/Cyril Ruoso/Bios; 26 Getty/Peter Arnold; 27 Getty/Bioshot; 28t Shutterstock/studiogi;
28b Getty/Martin Poole/The Image Bank; 29t Shutterstock/ George Filyagin; 29b Shutterstock/testbild;
30t Naturepl/Neil Bromhall; 30b FLPA/Mark Moffet/Minden; 31t Getty/Picture Press; 31b FLPA/Paul Hobson

Buzz!

What is that?

It is a bee!

Why does a bee buzz?

A bee is an **insect** with wings.

Its wings buzz when the bee flies.

This **honeybee** is busy.

She flies from flower
to flower.

She sips the flower's
nectar.

Munch, munch.

The bee chews the flower's **pollen**.

Pollen looks like a powder.

Some pollen sticks to the bee.

At the next flower, some pollen falls off the bee.

New flowers grow when
flowers share pollen.

This busy bee helps new flowers grow.

And she doesn't even know it!

The honeybee flies home.

Her home is called a **hive**.

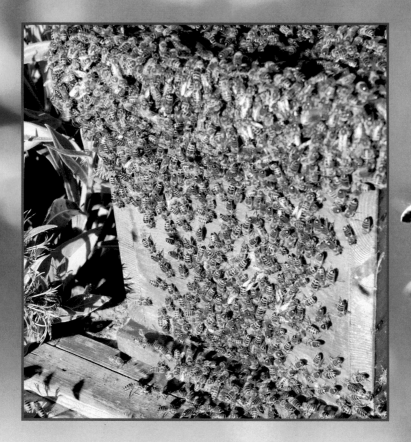

Many honeybees
share one hive.

Look!

The bee is still busy.

She wiggles.

She waggles.

The other bees watch.

What is she doing?

She is telling the other bees where to find food!

The hive is
a busy place!

Every bee
has a job.

The queen bee is the head bee.

She is the only honeybee
that lays eggs.

The queen bee is always in the hive.

She is the biggest bee.

Can you see her?

Worker bees take care of the queen.

They build rooms for her eggs too.

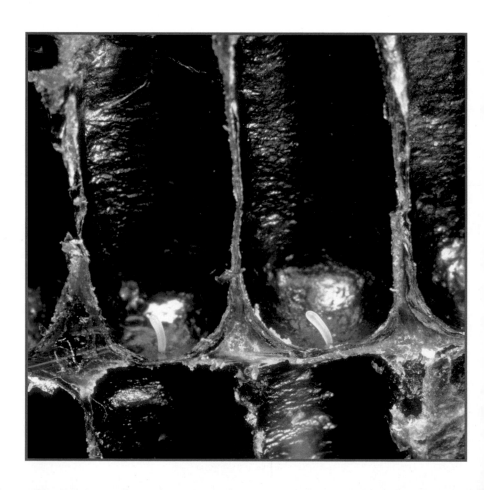

The rooms are made with
beeswax.

Honeybees make beeswax
inside their bodies!

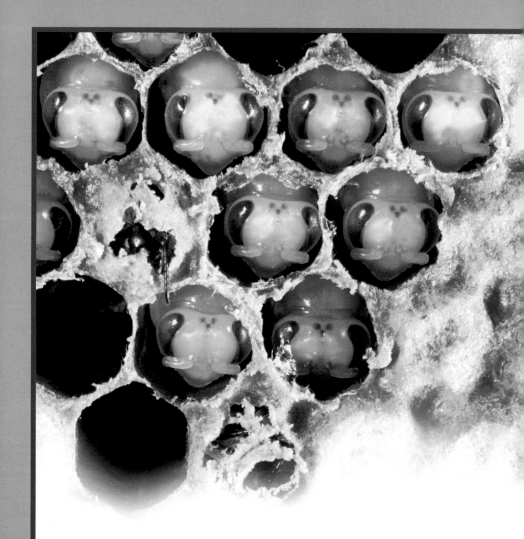

Each room has six sides.

Each room is for one egg.

The eggs **hatch** after three days.

But baby bees need
to keep growing.

Some worker bees
care for them
until they grow up.

Other worker bees
keep the hive safe.

They keep out bees and other
animals that do not belong.

They will sting
if they have to!

Some worker bees go
to get nectar.

They bring it back
for others to eat.

Honeybees save some nectar in the hive.

The nectar turns into **honey**.

The bees eat the honey.

We eat honey too.

It tastes sweet.

Do you
like honey?

We use beeswax too.

We use it
in crayons.

And we use it in candles.

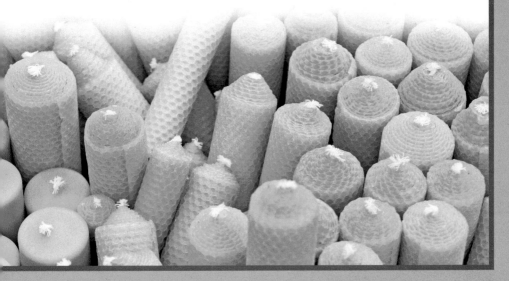

Bees are busy!

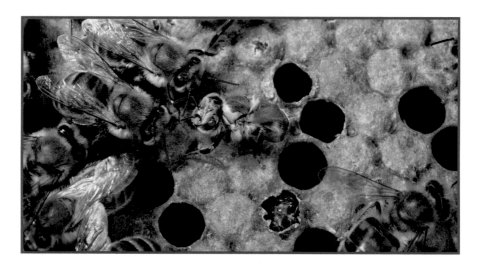

Some take care of baby bees.

Some bring food for other bees.

Some make honey and beeswax.

Bees help new flowers grow too.

Buzz!

Glossary

beeswax the wax honeybees make to build rooms in their hive

hatch to break out of an egg and be born

hive a home that a group of honeybees live in together

honey a sweet food that honeybees make from nectar

honeybee an insect that flies and makes honey

insect a small animal with six legs

nectar something sweet found in flowers that honeybees drink and use to make honey

pollen something powdery in flowers that is needed for new flowers to grow